Fly for Free

HOW TO EARN FREE FLIGHTS ACROSS THE US AND AROUND THE WORLD

SIGN UP FOR THE FREE UDEMY COURSE ACCOMPANYING THIS BOOK!

READ THIS FIRST

Just to say thanks for buying or downloading my book, I would like to give you access to the Udemy Course I am putting together 100% FREE!

In video form I will walk through how to look for the best deals, exactly what you should be looking out for in credit card offers, conversations I have with credit card companies when canceling my cards, and much more that I simply wouldn't be able to explain in a book.

This course will ONLY be free to purchasers of this book and will eventually be sold to the general public at $37. So be sure to sign up as being a buyer of this book.

(Go to: http://bitly.com/free-travel-course)

DISCLAIMER

I get ZERO benefit from you applying what I teach in this book.

Take or leave the information I give you.

My only desire with the book, other than a few book sales, is to show you how to travel the world with pennies on the dollar - just like I and many others featured in this book have done.

All results and people featured in this book are real.

No tricks and no gimmicks.

Nothing is meant to deceive you - only encourage you that cheap air travel is possible, and that it's more than just too good to be true.

I'm also not an advisor, nor am I giving you legal or financial advice.

Read through the book and do your research.

See if what is outlined in this book is right for you.

Maybe it is.

Maybe it isn't.

But only you can decide.

Best wishes and good luck.

Sincerely,
Pascal

(Riding on the back of a moped through rice fields in Bali, 2014)

All Results Featured In This Book Are Real

Dispersed throughout the book are biographies, direct quotes, and ways to reach out to each person who has implemented what is taught in this book.

Everything I teach you in this book, is real.

To add legitimacy and proof that I've done what I teach, I've included a video of my last around the world trip - only possible because of what I've written here.

If these biographies and the video don't get you jazzed about traveling the world, this book is not for you.

To check out the video, visit this web address:
http://bit.ly/pascal-around-the-world

Table Of Contents

Chapter 1: Introduction

Chapter 2: My Story

Chapter 3: How & Why This Works

Chapter 4: Will This Be Around Forever?

Chapter 5: How This Affects Your Credit Score

Chapter 6: Applying For Multiple Credit Cards Can Actually Improve Your Credit Score

Chapter 7: Insight & Stories From Other Travel Hackers

Chapter 8: How To Earn Miles

Chapter 9: How To Meet The Minimum Spending Requirements

Chapter 10: Which Credit Cards Transfer Points To Which Airline

Chapter 11: How To Keep Track Of Your Credit Cards & Miles

Chapter 12: How To Redeem Miles

Chapter 13: Where To Go To Find Costs For Upcoming Trips

Chapter 14: How To Cancel Credit Cards And Save Your Credit

Chapter 15: Next Steps & Resources

Chapter 16: It's Your Turn To Travel The World

CHAPTER 1
Introduction
How You Can Earn Frequent Flyer Miles To Travel The World.

When was the last time you flew across the world? Took a trip to Europe? Or how about took a vacation in Hawaii?

If you are anything like I was a couple years ago, you are itching to travel the world and see what it has to offer, but flights that cost thousands of dollars are stopping you in your tracks from reaching this dream.

Perhaps, like me, you want to walk in the footsteps of centuries-old civilization, slip into the bluest waters on our beautiful planet, and lick your fingers clean after tasting your first fried grasshopper in the packed streets of Thailand, but you have no idea how to get started.

If this is you (or if this has been you), I can tell you that I've been in your shoes. I've looked through every travel magazine and scoured *Lonely Planet* like nobody's business, dreaming of all the places I wanted to visit.

All I wanted was to get out of the United States and see the other 99% of the world I've been missing out on, but I just couldn't figure out how to get past paying the thousands of dollars for each flight.

I kept doing this until I discovered the art of Travel Hacking — beating the credit card and airline companies at their own game. It's a strategic way of using credit cards to earn frequent flyer miles and trading them in for free flights.

I know what you're thinking.

"Credit cards? That sounds too good to be true… Even then, won't applying for a bunch of credit cards ruin my credit score?"

Let me explain.

There's this ridiculous misconception out there that credit cards are "bad"-- that playing with credit cards will ruin your credit score and your financial life. And it's true — if you're reckless. If you don't pay off your credit card each month or do not pay attention to what you're spending, then yes, it will wreck your finances.

If you're like most people, though, chances are you're capable of managing the money you spend. If you do not go overboard, you have nothing to fear.

If anyone had these excuses, it was me.

It was in college that I began hearing about travel hacking from other students on campus. These people had traveled the world — they rode camels across the sand dunes in Egypt and swam with all of the colorful fish at the Great Barrier Reef. Needless to say my interest was piqued, but I just wrote off the possibility of earning free flights because I didn't know how applying for various cards would affect my credit.

I thought because I was so young (I started at 22) that my credit was fragile and that applying for numerous credit cards would destroy my credit. I understood that credit cards offered frequent flyer miles and you could exchange them for flights, but somehow I believed that credit card companies would keep an eye on me like Big Brother and prevent me from accumulating so many benefits.

A significant turning point in my life came after graduating college and moving to Boulder, Colorado. I decided if there was any time to try this, it would be now. I went from just reading about travel hacking passively on the internet, to taking the leap — feet first.

From then on, my life and the world of what I thought possible changed. Because of the experiences I've been able to have, and because of the amount of joy and fulfillment it's brought into my life, I wanted to take the same strategies I've used to travel the world and share them with you.

Just imagine — the travel you thought would not be possible is now at your fingertips. The ability to race camels between the pyramids in Egypt or to swim with the stingrays in Bali are now accessible for pennies on the dollar to you and me.

I wouldn't tell you anything that I haven't tried myself. As you'll read later I've flown to Hawaii to swim with the sea turtles, surfed the ten foot waves off the coast of Bali, and have eaten God knows what in Hong Kong. But I imagine that my word alone might not convince you. That's why I encourage you to read through the following profiles scattered throughout the book, and reach out to them to get their honest feedback about their travel hacking experience.

MAX NACHAMKIN

Before I took the leap I had the fear of not being able to manage all of my credit cards correctly. I kept asking myself "Won't it negatively affect my credit score?". Pushing my fears aside and applying for two additional credit cards I not only received over 100,000 frequent flyer miles but my credit score has actually gone up from around 737 to ~780.

For the last year I've been able to fly in the US for free. 3x to San Diego. 2x to Philly to see my family. And it allowed me to host my Dating for Entrepreneurs retreat in a location across the country all without spending a dime on travel.

If you have any questions for me, reach out to me on twitter: @MaxN

In this book I'm going to give you the keys to my step-by-step travel hacking formula, so you too can start enjoying the same benefits that I discovered.

I will tell you this: In 90 days you can earn enough frequent flyer miles to lounge on the beach in Hawaii, dine in the streets of New York, or walk along the piers of San Francisco — and pay less than $10 for the flight.

That's all it takes. Less than 90 days.

It's the exact blueprint that my friends and I have used to fly to many different places around the globe.

I've tested, tweaked, and perfected this formula.

If you follow what I'm about to lay out, you will earn enough miles to earn your first free flight or (depending on how far down the rabbit hole you go) travel the world within your first year.

I know it seems too good to be true, but no matter your age, how little you currently travel, or how much you spend each month, this formula will work for you. As long as you're not knee-deep in debt and have decent credit (above 600), I can show you how to become a frequent traveler and earn flights around the globe for pennies on the dollar.

Don't be the person who misses out on this opportunity because you brush off these kinds of stories as "too good to be true". Be the kind of person other people marvel at. Be the kind of person other people see and say, "I don't know how they do it." Be the kind of person who takes action.

What I reveal in this book is the approach that millions of Americans overlook but a select few use to travel the world and live out their dreams.

In the next chapter, I'll start by telling you how frequent flyer miles completely changed my life. Then I'll get to the good stuff by laying out my step-by-step formula and showing you how you too can travel the world.

If you're ready to see how you can travel the world for less than the price of movie tickets, then read on.

CHAPTER 2
My Story

In January 2013, I applied for my first credit card with no real idea what I was doing. I had just moved to Colorado, and one of the first friends I made was Shane Rasnak. He was a normal guy in his 20's, had studied at Cornell and was now working at a startup.

When we first met, we sat down and talked about what we had been working on, our values, and what it meant to live a meaningful life. (An intense first-time conversation, I know.) We were sharing traveling stories when he casually mentioned that he was leaving for Colombia the next day to work remotely for one month — for $10.

I was FLOORED.

I remember reading how to acquire frequent flyer miles using credit cards just a couple months before, but was always too shy and fearful to actually pull the trigger. I thought that because I was young, I didn't have the necessary income to apply for credit and credit cards. At that point, I didn't even know what credit was.

This whole idea of applying for credit cards and getting frequent flyer miles so that I could fly for dirt cheap all of a sudden became very real. This guy sitting next to me was flying the next day to Colombia for a whopping $10. I absolutely couldn't believe it. For perspective, that's less than a meal at Chipotle if you order guacamole.

I asked Shane if he would guide me through the process of starting to travel hack before he left. He agreed, and that day we sat down together and went online to search for a credit card that would give me 50,000 frequent flyer miles. My heart pounded because I didn't really know what would happen to my credit score or my financial future. But I had done my research and knew that I had put this off longer than I should have. I finally decided to take the leap.

Within one week I had my first credit card and started travel hacking.

That card was the first step that would take me from dreaming about galavanting across the earth to actually seeing countries I never thought I'd visit. From there, the world opened up for me.

My first "free" trip I ever took was to Hawaii in January of 2014. On a Thursday I went snowboarding in Keystone, Colorado, and then Friday I was lying on a beach in Maui. It was like a dream. For my trip from Denver to Hawaii I spent a total of $10 in taxes and 37,500 frequent flyer miles.

From then on, I was hooked. I tried applying for as many cards as I could.

I used air miles to fly to Los Angeles for a dance festival. Total cost: $5 and 18,251 miles.

Then there was a business conference I wanted to attend but previously couldn't afford traveling to. Total cost: $8 and 12,000 miles.

I flew to weddings across the country. I went to business conferences on the east and west coasts. And I took spontaneous weekend getaways to Florida for less than the cost of a pair of sandals.

I then started to realize that I could use my miles more strategically and take flights that would cost me a fortune (especially during the holiday season).

In December 2014, I flew home for Christmas from Denver to Florida. A round trip that would have cost me $850 ended up being $20 and 40,000 frequent flyer miles.

Trip after trip, I visited different places across the United States and around the world at a fraction of the cost.

My favorite trip of them all: I saved enough frequent flyer miles to afford an around-the-world ticket.

In the summer of 2014 I flew from Denver to London, Germany, Bali, Thailand, Hong Kong, Australia, Los Angeles and then back to Denver. It was the trip of a lifetime. I applied for 3 credit cards amounting to over 150,000 points. The entire trip cost me $633 and 140,000 miles.

633 dollars. That's it.

A typical around-the-world ticket would cost you $2,700 to $10,000, making $633 a steal.

I sometimes still can't believe how all of this was possible. At the time of this writing, I've racked up 10 (nearly) free flights. And here's my Excel tracking sheet to show it.

Trip	Starting Location	Ending Location	# of Stops	Airline	Miles	Cost
Hawaii Trip	DEN	OGG	1	United Airlines	20,000	$5.00
	OGG	DEN	3	American Airlines	17,500	$5.00
				Trip Total	**37,500**	**$10.00**
LA Zouk Congress	DEN	LAX	0	Southwest	9,251	$5.00
	LAX	DEN	0	Southwest	9,000	$0.00
				Trip Total	**18,251**	**$5.00**
Around The World	DEN			American Airlines	140,000	$633.20
		DEN				$0.00
				Trip Total	**140,000**	**$633.20**
MetaMind	DEN	PHX	0	Southwest	5,000	$8.00
	PHX	DEN	0	Southwest	7,000	$0.00
				Trip Total	**12,000**	**$8.00**
Jeff's Wedding	DEN	PIT	0	Southwest	10,000	$0.00
	PIT	DEN	0	Southwest	10,000	$5.00
				Trip Total	**20,000**	**$5.00**
Florida Weekend	DEN	SRQ	1	Delta	20,000	$5.00
	SRQ	DEN	1	Delta	20,000	$5.00
				Trip Total	**40,000**	**$10.00**
Burning Man	DEN	RNO	0	United Airlines	25,000	$0.00
	RNO	DEN	0	United Airlines	25,000	$11.20
				Trip Total	**50,000**	**$11.20**
Christmas (FL)	DEN	SRQ	2	Delta	25,000	$0.00
	SRQ	DEN	2	Delta	25,000	$11.20
				Trip Total	**50,000**	**$11.20**
Tony Robbins	DEN	LGA	0	Southwest	7,424	$5.50
	LGA	DEN	0	Southwest	7,424	$5.50
				Trip Total	**14,848**	**$11.00**
Unity Dance Festival	DEN	TPA	0	Southwest	10,484	$5.60
	TPA	DEN	0	Southwest	10,484	$5.60
				Trip Total	**20,968**	**$11.00**
				Grand Total	403,567	$715.60
				Travelhacked Trips	10	

Over the next couple chapters, I'll outline how and why it all works — and how you can go about doing the exact same thing.

CHAPTER 3
How & Why This Works

Virtually every company that interacts with the mass of consumers has some sort of loyalty program — your grocery store, hotel chains, car rental companies, and of course, airlines. Look in your wallet or purse. Do you participate in the rewards program at your nearby supermarket? Have you ever received coupons in your email or use any apps on your phone to give you discounts? Why do we participate in these loyalty or discount programs?

It's to save money, of course. As the blogger, Lucky, from One Mile At A Time states:

> *We offer our loyalty and consistent patronage to a business, and in exchange they reward us with better prices, discounts, special offers, and other things that make us feel like a valued customer.*

While to the consumer these loyalty programs look like a way for these companies to reward their frequent customers, they are in fact huge assets that companies use as tools to keep us coming back for more.

Take for example the airline industry's rewards programs — the psychological benefit of earning and using frequent flyer miles is so great that many people will take an extra connection or even pay more for tickets to fly their preferred airlines. The airlines understand this psychological desire very well, and they go to great lengths to get as many people to buy into it with heavy advertising. This is why you see airline miles offered as benefits on the backbone to the American economy — credit.

Don't believe that the hundreds of millions of unused frequent flyer miles are a liability to the airline or the industry. These companies would not be trying so hard to get millions of Americans to acquire these miles if it worked against their best interest.

Makes you think a little differently about loyalty programs, doesn't it?

Unfortunately, most people are unaware of how these frequent flyer loyalty programs work, and therefore not many take advantage of what the programs have to offer. To make it worse, in many cases airlines create restrictions that prevent the average person from redeeming their hard-earned frequent flyer miles for the travel they were promised.

Here's how most people travel:

They plan a vacation around specific dates -- especially holidays. Many times it is around these dates that either the miles are the most expensive to redeem or cannot be redeemed at all.

This happens to my parents on a regular basis. They have well over 180,000 points just sitting in an account waiting to be used. Their travel arrangements for every trip that they plan somehow do not fall within the redemption guidelines of frequent flyer programs. Thus, all the free travel they were promised with their credit cards or the airlines is out the window.

On top of this, reward seat availability is subject to black-out dates and seasonal fluctuations, as airlines use all kinds of statistics and big data to calculate the number of seats people like us can book using our frequent flyer miles. The rewards that credit card companies use to lure us into applying for credit are the same ones that the airline companies place restrictions around. So these rewards are seldom used.

I'm not as against the airlines as it sounds. Without them we wouldn't be able to galavant across the world. However, their loyalty programs are structured in a way to mislead people who don't know any better.

And to my point, because of the way these frequent flyer programs are set up, it's only fair for us to do everything we can to make these points work in our favor. This means we should earn as many points as we can and learn how to redeem them for high-value trips that would otherwise be very expensive.

How do we do this? It's simple: figure out how many points we need to take a certain trip, earn those points easily by applying for credit cards, and cancel the cards before they get us into financial trouble. Everything is legal and uses the various incentive systems the companies have set up to our benefit.

CHAPTER 4
Will This Be Around Forever?

Do I think credit card companies will stop offering these deals because of the publishing of this book?

In reality, no.

The art of travel hacking has been around for years.

The thing is, the number of people who actually take advantage of what I lay before you is really small. We're talking far less than one percent of all air travelers.

And this is great for credit card companies. Many of the people I know applied for cards with the idea of getting rid of them in a year or two and in the end have decided to keep them long-term. Take for example my buddy Nate…

NATE BLEADORN

When I first started I looked into the Southwest travel card. I applied and used it for the 50,000 mile bonus after spending $3k in the first 3 months. I basically met the minimum spending requirement by charging rent to my card.

Now I travel almost exclusively Southwest for work and personal trips. I also keep in contact with Southwest through their customer service email. I let them know when I have troubles, and I let them know when I had a flawless travel experience. I have received milage or monetary credit (through what they call a "LUV Voucher") in both instances.

I also routinely ask for upgraded boarding positions (since there is no "First Class" on SWA) and free drink tickets, and lots of times get them. I have also stayed late on a trip because of overbooked flights and received vouchers to the tune of just over $1,000 last year. I then received points from booking the travel that was already free.

Ask about my travel experiences on twitter: @Bleadorn

In other scenarios people rack up a bunch of credit card debt and don't end up paying it off each month. That is exactly the goal of credit card companies: they hope to collect enough interest from those who cannot pay off their debt each month to make up for the rewards they give out.

I seriously can't say this enough: PAY OFF YOUR CREDIT CARD EACH MONTH!

Will the ability to rack up frequent flyer miles for flights be around forever?

I don't know.

Would you be able to rack up enough points for an around-the-world tour or a few domestic flights this first year?

Hell yes.

And you should do it now, because the train will definitely leave the station one day or another. Heck, in December 2014 Delta stopped allowing the use of points for around-the-world tickets. That program had been around for years, but things change, so take advantage of these programs while you still can.

CHAPTER 5
How This Affects Your Credit Score

One of the most common questions or objections I get when it comes to opening multiple credit cards in order to earn frequent flyer miles is:

"Doesn't that hurt your credit score?"

The short answer is no.

Now, I've heard of people's credit scores dropping.

Do I know why *their* credit score dropped? No.

Do I think it's directly from travel hacking? Maybe.

There *are* risks with applying for multiple credit cards, and I cover that in detail in the following paragraphs. But that's why you have to understand how the credit game works.

Most people don't understand what goes into your credit score, and because they don't know how it works they automatically reject using this travel hacking strategy altogether.

That being said, if my formula ruined credit scores, you'd better believe I would not be doing it — and neither would the thousands of other travel hackers out there. Our credit scores are too important to just throw out the window for a few free flights around the globe.

Before diving into how this works into your credit score, you may be asking yourself "What exactly is credit?" Below is a great explanation from the FICO website of what credit is:

Whether you're buying a home, a car or applying for a credit card – lenders want to know the risk they're taking by lending you money. FICO® Scores are the credit scores used by 90% of top lenders to determine your credit risk. Your FICO® Scores (you have FICO® Scores for each of the 3 major bureaus) can affect how much money a lender will lend you and at what terms (interest rate). Higher FICO® Scores can often help you qualify for better rates from lenders – which can save you money!

Now that you know what credit is, let's dive into the composition of a credit score and how it is calculated. FICO (the company that measures consumer credit risk) discloses the composition of all credit scores, and the breakdown looks like this:

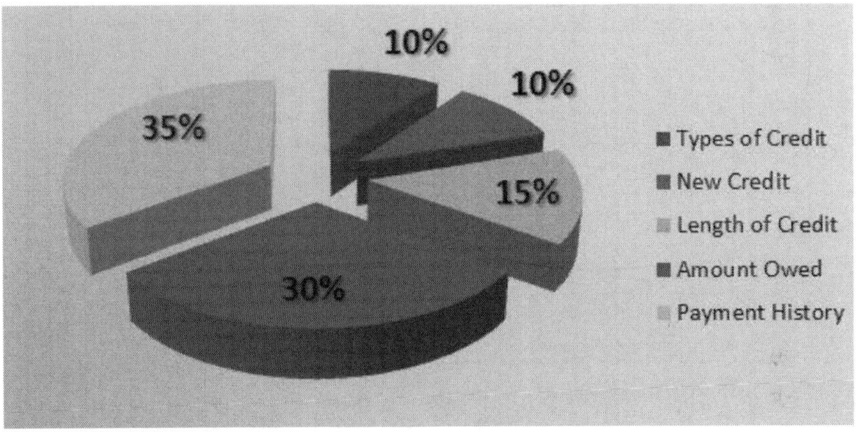

35%: Payment history

Late payments on bills will cause a FICO score to drop. Timely payments will improve a FICO score.

30%: Credit utilization

In other words, the percent of credit being used, or current debt owed divided by the total credit available. Opening new lines of credit, paying off debt, or receiving a credit line increase will all increase available credit, lower the credit utilization ratio, and therefore increase a FICO score. Less debt means a higher score.

15%: Length of credit history

This can include average age of all credit accounts, and also individual relationships with each lender.

10%: Types of credit

Having diverse types of credit, including installment, revolving, consumer finance, and mortgages, will improve a FICO score.

10%: Recent searches for credit

Too many hard credit inquiries, which occur when applying for a credit card or loan, can temporarily hurt a FICO score.

You'll notice that only 10% of your credit score is affected by recent credit inquiries, such as credit card applications. This is vitally important, because many people are terrified of opening up several new credit cards. They believe that new credit card applications will just destroy a credit score, which is just not true.

In fact, the official FICO website actually has a section dedicated to "facts and fallacies" surrounding credit scores:

> Fallacy: "My score will drop if I apply for new credit".
>
> Fact: If it does, it probably won't drop by much. If you apply for several credit cards within a short period of time, multiple requests for your credit report information (called "inquiries") will appear on your report. Looking for new credit can equate with higher risk, but most credit scores are not affected by multiple inquiries from auto or mortgage lenders within a short period of time. Typically, these are

treated as a single inquiry and will have little impact on the credit score.

CHAPTER 6

Applying For Multiple Credit Cards Can Actually Improve Your Credit Score

In other words, applying for multiple credit cards can initially have a minor negative impact on your credit score. However, over time these new lines of credit can actually *improve* the other, more heavily weighted factors of your credit score.

As mentioned above, 30% is determined by credit utilization. When you are approved for more credit, your overall available credit increases. All else equal, more available credit will decrease your credit utilization ratio and increase your credit score over time.

Opening multiple cards also allows you to establish a longer credit history as each account ages. And if you pay the monthly balance in full, you'll continue to build trustworthiness and a solid payment history with each account. As the years roll on, you'll build great relationships with each bank and have an excellent payment history record.

So even if your score does slightly decrease after a few new applications, it will inevitably rebound and continue moving higher over time.

So far I have not had any issues with any banks. I've even applied for mortgages and had them approved after going through 9 credit cards.

That being said, it would be naive of me to think it's all sunshine and rainbows. None of the following has happened to me, but the potential downsides are:

- Issuers could ban you from applying for new credit. Credit card issuers are well aware of the existence of applying for cards and cancelling them by the end of the year. They may choose to ban you, either temporarily or permanently, from applying for credit cards or receiving signup bonuses.

- Credit card management can be overwhelming. It can be difficult to manage multiple credit accounts, and there is always the risk you'll miss payments or overspend in order to hit the spending requirements to receive travel bonuses.

- Each new account will shorten your average account age. This is why it's risky to do this too much without a long credit history. For instance, if you have one credit account you opened five years ago and decide to open one more account today, your average credit age will decrease to two-and-a-half years. This is a significant drop and will likely hurt your credit score.

- Closing accounts can increase utilization. If you carry revolving debt, closing credit accounts will increase your credit utilization, possibly decreasing your credit score. Let's say you have one previous credit card with a limit of $5,000 and a balance of $3,000, and then you cancel a card with a limit of $5,000, but don't carry a balance. In this case, you are currently utilizing 30% of your credit ($3,000/$10,000), which most experts say is acceptable. However, if you close the second account, your utilization is now 60%. This is high enough for potential creditors to see you as a risk, so your credit score will likely drop.

- People with a shorter credit history (or those who are in their early 20's) are going to be affected more by having more credit inquiries on their record.

- If you have a lot of credit cards and you close an account, your credit has the possibility of taking a hit.

You may be asking yourself the question, "How many credit cards can you have at one time?". And all of this comes down to your personal preference. I've had five credit cards open at a time, and it's not uncommon to hear of other people doing the same thing. The photo below just highlights how its pretty common to have multiple cards (These photos may be dated but you can find much of the same information at FlyerTalk.com).

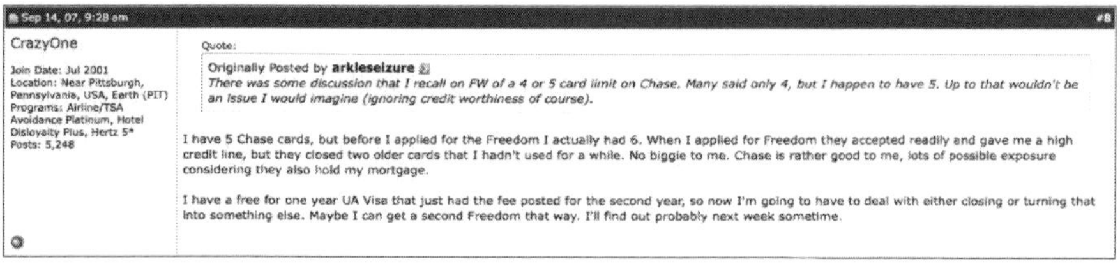
Sep 14, 07, 9:28 am #8

CrazyOne

Join Date: Jul 2001
Location: Near Pittsburgh, Pennsylvania, USA, Earth (PIT)
Programs: Airline/TSA Avoidance Platinum, Hotel Disloyalty Plus, Hertz 5*
Posts: 5,248

Quote:

Originally Posted by **arkleseizure**
There was some discussion that I recall on FW of a 4 or 5 card limit on Chase. Many said only 4, but I happen to have 5. Up to that wouldn't be an issue I would imagine (ignoring credit worthiness of course).

I have 5 Chase cards, but before I applied for the Freedom I actually had 6. When I applied for Freedom they accepted readily and gave me a high credit line, but they closed two older cards that I hadn't used for a while. No biggie to me. Chase is rather good to me, lots of possible exposure considering they also hold my mortgage.

I have a free for one year UA Visa that just had the fee posted for the second year, so now I'm going to have to deal with either closing or turning that into something else. Maybe I can get a second Freedom that way. I'll find out probably next week sometime.

I recommend you read into the facts instead of the myths that exist. Here are some additional resources that have proved to be useful:

- http://bit.ly/frugal-travel-rookie
- http://bit.ly/improve-credit-score
- http://bit.ly/freakin-flyers-beginners
- http://bit.ly/lifehacker-multiple-credit-cards

CHAPTER 7

Insight & Stories From Other Travel Hackers

JUSTIN TAYEZZ

I began travel hacking in June 2013 and as of this writing I've visited over 26 countries. When I first started, I was scared of ending up some place and getting stuck. With no job, no local contacts, and no money sometimes, I thought it was inevitable sooner or later. So far, it's never happened, people have always been kind enough to extend help to travelers in unfamiliar territory.

If you have any questions, feel free to reach out to me on instagram: @tayezz

JULES SCHROEDER

Unlike a lot of people who get into travel hacking my fears were that it wasn't going to be worth my time. I feared that I wouldn't have the flexibility that I wanted in booking flights, that I would have to fly at odd hours of the night or that the quality of my trips would diminish.

Fortunately that wasn't true. Although at the beginning I found myself slightly overwhelmed figuring out which cards to apply for and how to manage them, once I got my foundation set up it's been a no brainer ever since.

I've been travel hacking for over two years and now have a system where I basically earn and use one new flight every month. Because of this strategy I haven't paid for a domestic flight in over a year.

If you have questions for me, definitely reach out to me on twitter: @hijulesandchris

VICTOR CORTES

Travel hacking never really crossed my mind until I started traveling for work. Once I started traveling once a week, sometimes more, for work; I noticed all of the credit card offers I began receiving. Each airline company had amazing offers to lure me into their frequent flyer program. I realized I could join all of them and reap the benefits along the way.

In the short year of signing up for the programs, I have planned trips to Napa Valley, LA, Dallas, Atlanta, and even Cairo, Egypt, for almost nothing. None of these trips would have been made possible without travel hacking. As long as you're responsible with the credit cards, there is no going wrong.

If you have any questions shoot me an email:
cortes.j.victor@gmail.com

ALEXI PANOS

I started travel hacking when I was 16 years old….by accident. I got an offer for my first credit card, which I took to help build my credit. I put a down payment for my first car on that card, and paid it off within the month, then closed the card. Within a week I had 4 other offers….this time, with travel points. So I repeated that cycle of opening cards, meeting the minimum spend with purchases I was planning on making, then paying it off; meanwhile racking up points.

Because I didn't get into this knowingly, I didn't have any fears. What fear transpired afterwards was: how can I keep up this spending without going into debt on things I don't need? I became pretty crafty with my spending and put all my monthly expenses on my card, or the cash advance "checks" they sent—including my pricey NYC rent. Since then, my hacking ways have evolved…but I can't divulge all my secrets here!

I've traveled to over 65 countries, flown (at as little as 2 hours notice) to some amazing places….for a day or two, and it's afforded me the luxury of taking my business of creating conscious content (through YouTube videos and writings) to some amazing locations. I also get to say "YES!" to meetings and conferences all over the world without having to think twice about the ticket or hotel cost. Visiting family is never an issue, and I'm crossing so many places off my bucket list I'm having to make multiple lists! I'm living a lifestyle most people can't even fathom—and I'm spending the same (or less!) than what I would be spending if I were at home in Los Angeles.

If you're curious to hear more, hit me up @alexipanos

SHANE RASNAK

In all honesty I wasn't all that concerned when I started, I just went ahead and tried it. Something I did was I made sure that I checked my credit score every year with freecreditreport.com and mint.com. I've never missed a payment so its never done anything to my credit score and it is still considered excellent after 6 years of travel hacking.

What has it allowed me to do? I think in the last 5 or 6 years since I started I don't think I've ever paid a full fare for a flight. I've been to Columbia, New York, Japan, Thailand and Hawaii multiple times. I've also used it for a trip to Brazil for a remote work vacation for two weeks. It's just given me a lot of amazing experiences.

And in terms of meeting the minimum spending requirements, I would get a second card allocated for my mom to use and have her use it for all of her purchases. At the end of each month, I'd tally her expenses up and then have her send me a check. That alone has allowed me to reach $5,000 in the first three months in minimum spend.

If you have any questions, definitely reach out to me on twitter: @shanerasnak

RACHEL TENENBAUM YUGER

When I first started I thought that this travel hacking would be hard to figure out and that it would be too much to handle. I used to see friends and colleagues getting free flights and upgrades and was always so frustrated that I didn't get them. Finally I got fed up and decided to find a way to leverage all of my spending and travelling to be able to do it too.

With just a little bit of research and jumping in 100%, I've been able to enjoy the benefits of flying for free just about anywhere I want to go. I use my points to upgrade to economy plus every time I fly for the extra leg room and it's allowed me to see all of my friends across the country. Now I never have to worry about missing a retreat, conference or event and flights and travel have become a fun game for me to enjoy life!

Reach out to me on twitter if you have any questions: @SHSocialite

CHAPTER 8

How To Earn Miles

Figuring out which credit cards to apply for and exactly how to earn your free flights can get a bit overwhelming.

Earning miles is as simple as applying for a credit card that has a great offer. Like I mentioned earlier, the biggest misconception is that to earn frequent flyer miles, you must pay for flights and actually fly.

The truth is that the biggest number of flights and flyer miles are given out because of credit card *applications.*

Before I tell you where to find the best credit cards, I've dug up a few good example offers to show you what to look for.

CHASE
SAPPHIRE
PREFERRED
D. BARRETT
Chase Sapphire Preferred® Card
40,000 BONUS POINTS
when you spend $4,000 on purchases in the first 3 months from account opening* -
That's $500 in travel when you redeem through Chase Ultimate Rewards℠
• Earn 5,000 bonus points after you add the first authorized user and make a purchase in the first 3 months from account opening.*
• Earn 2X points on travel and dining at restaurants and 1 point per dollar spent on all other purchases.*
• 1:1 point transfer to leading frequent travel programs at a full 1:1 value - that means 1,000 Chase Ultimate Rewards points equal 1,000 partner miles/points.
• Always get 20% off travel when you redeem for airfare, hotel stays, car rentals and cruises through Chase Ultimate Rewards. For example, a $500 flight requires just 40,000 points.
• Pay no foreign transaction fees* when you use your card on purchases made outside the United States.
• Embedded Chip and Signature feature allows you to use your card for chip-based purchases when traveling outside the United States, while still allowing you to use your card as you do at home.
• 24/7 direct access to dedicated customer service advisors.
• Introductory Annual Fee of $0 the first year, then $95.*

Something to note is that when looking for cards online, different websites will offer different bonuses. You'll notice that the same card will offer a bonus of 30,000 miles on one website and 40,000 miles on a different website.

The amount you need to spend in order to redeem the purchase in the first 3 months also tends to vary. In the photo above you'll notice that you need to spend $4,000 in the first 3 months, whereas when I applied for this card I only needed to spend $3,000 and I still received the same amount of miles.

Let's look at another offer.

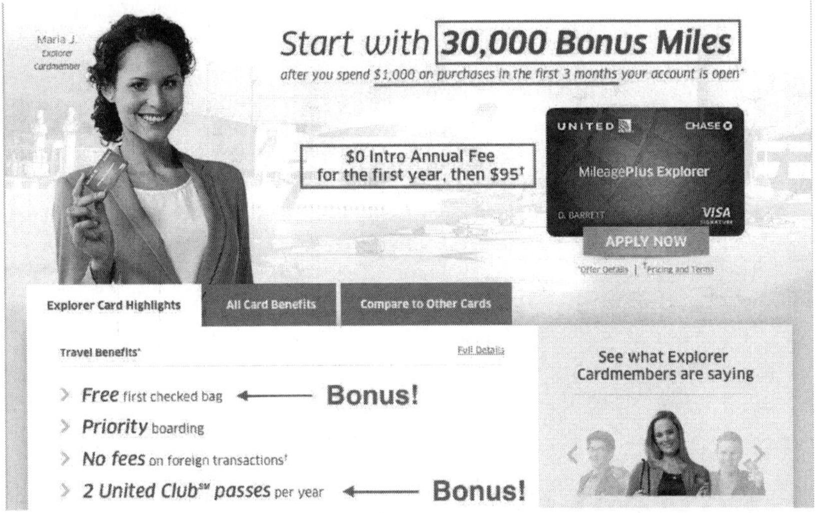

On this card you'd receive 30,000 in bonus points, but you only need to spend $1,000 within 90 days. In addition you get free checked bags and United Club passes (which means you get to enjoy a lounge with free food, drinks and alcoholic beverages!).

Each card and bonus will vary, so it is worth looking into which cards offer the best bonuses. But it's definitely not something you should squint over for longer than 20 minutes.

In case this is a little confusing for you, as a supplement to the book I'm creating a course on Udemy that should help you out. In video form I will walk through how to look for the best deals, exactly what you should be looking out for in credit card offers, conversations I have with credit card companies when canceling my cards and much more that I simply wouldn't be able to explain in a book.

If you think that will be useful, go to: http://bitly.com/free-travel-course to sign up.

(The course will be free for you as a purchaser of this book but be sold to the general public at $37)

CHAPTER 9
How To Meet The Minimum Spending Requirements

In the beginning I had three new cards and had to spend over $6,000 in the first three months, so I got creative. I tried…

- **Buying all of my roommates' groceries and having them pay me back.** When I first started travel hacking and I had to meet the minimum spending requirements, I would go to the grocery story once a week and offer to pick up groceries for my four roommates (then I'd have them pay me back in cash). Worked like a charm.

- **Pay for dinner on your card and have your friends pay you in cash.** Occasionally I went out to dinner with a big group of friends, maybe 10, and at the end I would ask if I could pay for the bill on my credit card and then have my friends pay me in cash, or paypal/venmo it to me. I have to say it was a bit of a hassle, but hey — if you just need to meet the minimum spending requirement, then it's worth doing once or twice (especially if it's a big bill).

- **Pay for trips and have your friends refund you.** I've taken several trips out of state, including a road trip to Glacier National Park in Montana and weekend vacations with the guys. Every time, I have offered to pay for everything using my card and then would show the tally at the end of the trip. This actually proved pretty useful because we weren't worried about who paid for what. Rather, we had all of the expenses on one credit card (mine of course) and we could split the total evenly between all of us.

Other than those few things, I really haven't had to get that creative. If you think about it, you probably already spend a minimum of $400 per month on food, $50/mo on utilities, and $100/mo in gas. That's basically $1,500 in your first three months right there.

This doesn't take into account any time you go to the bar, the movies, or buy anything from Amazon. You shouldn't be spending money you don't need to in order to reach the bonus amount. By thinking about HOW you are paying for things, and trying a few of these tricks, you will likely be able to hit your goal without bringing on any crazy expenses. In reality, reaching the minimum spending requirement isn't that difficult. And just to drive the point home, here are some other stories of travel hackers who might have had the same thoughts as you:

LACEY ANKENMAN

Travel hacking was a hard sell for me. I was worried that I didn't know enough about the process, and I'd make a mistake that would hurt my credit score. I finally took the leap – I ordered a card and soon booked my first free flight to New York. Since then, I've used miles for round trip tickets to Florida and London.

Researching and managing the cards does take some time, but for me it's worth it. Since I'm using everyday expenses to earn miles, I don't feel guilty about booking flights, so I inherently travel more. And I can use the money I save on flights for adventures in new places.

If you have any questions, reach out to me on Twitter: @LaceyDesign

DIEGO CORZO

One of my fears that I had in the beginning was that I didn't think I was going to be able to meet the minimum spending requirement in the first three months. Somehow I always managed to do it — whether it was paying for my roommates and they paid me back in cash or things for my parents. Also any expenses I knew I was going to have in the future I would just pay ahead of time.

Since I've started travel hacking I've flown to Florida twice, Nevada, Colorado, Ohio, Philadelphia, and Chicago.

Never again will I have the issue of wanting to hangout with my friends for the weekend in Florida and then having to save $400 just so I can fly out and visit them. Have any questions? Tweet at me: @DiegoCorzo

In case you apply for a couple of credit cards at once and you need to meet a higher spending requirement in your first couple of months (like $4,000-$6,000), here's a list of ways to go about meeting it.

For legal reasons (and because I haven't tried these), I can't go into too much depth here but below are a few resources for what can be considered "point laundering" methods of reaching the minimum spending requirements.

- Buying Gift Cards - http://bit.ly/buying-gift-cards
- Amazon Payments - http://bit.ly/amazon-payments
- Buying Prepaid Cards - http://bit.ly/buying-prepaid-cards
- Additional Manufactured Spending - http://bit.ly/manufactured-spending

I've also put together a list of methods you could use to reach your minimum spend if you absolutely couldn't find other ways of reaching the minimum spend wanted to but this list almost defeats the purpose of obtaining frequent flyer miles because of the extra fees you'll pay. In the spirit of travel hacking, you wouldn't want to pay the extra fees associated with purchasing these with your credit card, as then your cheap travel isn't actually cheap.

Paying $30/mo for your mortgage/rent or incurring fees through paypal to pay employees would actually cost you quite a bit of money over a year. We're talking a minimum of $500, and for that price you could buy a flight instead of using miles for it. It's a personal preference I guess, but I've heard of plenty people doing it.

Here's the list:

- Pay your mortgage with your credit card
- Paying rent with your credit through a service like - http://www.rentpayment.com

- Pay your taxes with a credit card - http://bit.ly/irs-taxes
- Or pay for any other cash or non-credit card allowed expense through paypal (and incur a 1-3% fee)

CHAPTER 10

Which Credit Cards Transfer Points To Which Airline

This is something I wish I knew when I first started!

I originally thought that as long as I got points within the same air alliance that I would be able to transfer points amongst airlines.

Wrong.

Not only that, but transferring points from person to person also can cost a serious amount of cash, depending on what accounts and carriers you are trying to make the trades from.

For example, when I tried booking my first around-the-world ticket with American Airlines, we tried to see if my parents could transfer a good chunk of their unused points to my account. It would have cost between $500-$1,200 to transfer between 30,000 and 180,000 points.

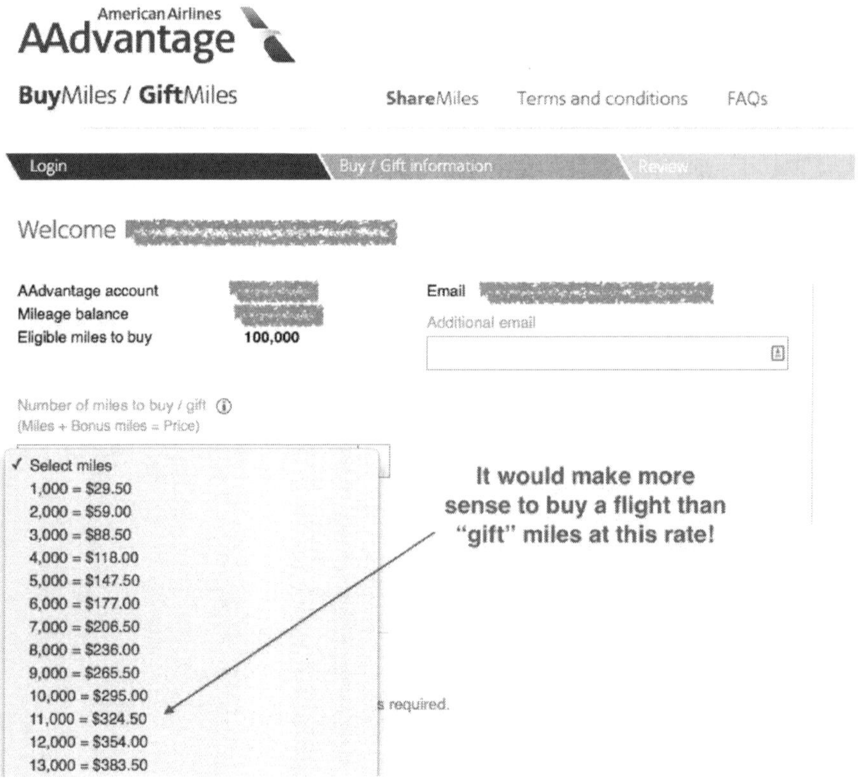

Forget that. I might as well buy the flight at that point.

But with American Express and Chase Bank you can transfer your points to anyone without a fee. So if you have a significant other or a good buddy you can put together all of your points in one account.

Below I have two photos that show you which credit card companies allow you to transfer points to other airlines.

American Express

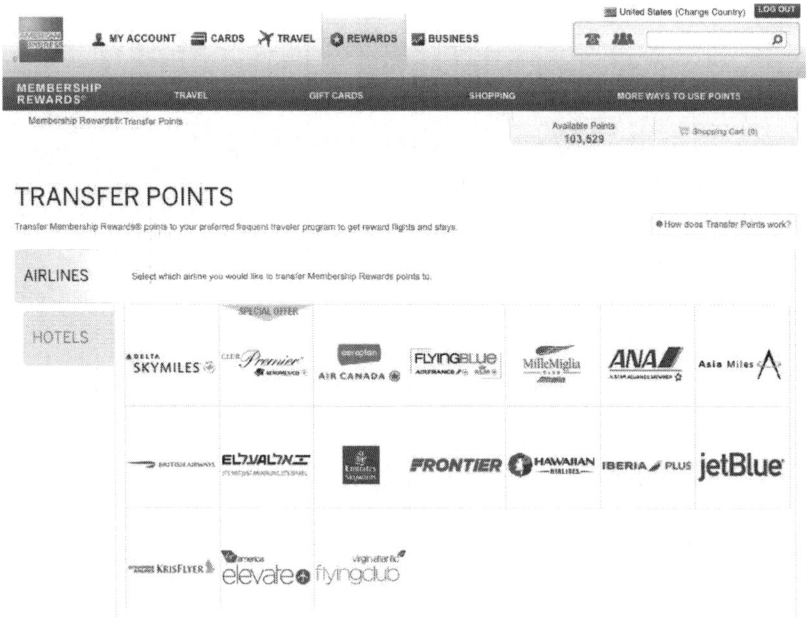

Any Chase-Related Credit Card

What this means is that if you earn points with American Express you can transfer those points to more than 17 different carriers as of the writing of this book.

And if you earn points with Chase, you can transfer them to a different set of airlines and hotels.

Don't make the mistake of thinking you can earn points on your Chase credit cards and your American Express and transfer them all to the same airline. You can't.

CHAPTER 11
How To Keep Track Of Your Credit Cards & Miles

Here is a spreadsheet I use to keep track of just a few of my credit cards and frequent flyer miles that I use every time I make a decision about applying for a new card or canceling an existing one. It's simply an Excel file that lets me track when I applied for cards and when I need to cancel them by if I don't want to incur the annual fee. I'll dig into that and how to cancel your credit cards in a later chapter.

Previous Cards & Promotions	Card	Alliance	Projected Miles	Minimum Payment	1st Yr (Annual Fee)	Annual Fee	Fee Waivable?	Date Applied	Date Cancelled
US Airways Dividend Miles	?	Star Alliance	30,000	$1	$89	$89	N	3/12/2013	9/8/2013
Chase Ink Bold Business Card	Chase	Star Alliance	50,000	$5,000	$0	$95	n/a	3/12/2013	12/4/2013
United Milaege Plus Explorer	Chase	Star Alliance	35,000	$1,000	$0	$95	n/a	5/28/2013	6/10/2014
AAdvantage Card	Citi	OneWorld	30,000	$1,000	$0	$95	n/a	5/28/2013	6/10/2014
British Airways Visa Signature	Chase	OneWorld	50,000	$2,000	$0	$95	n/a	9/24/2013	9/23/2014
Southwest Rapid Rewards	Chase	N/A	50,000	$2,000	$99	$99	N	11/17/2013	11/14/2014
Chase Saphire Preferred	Chase	Star Alliance	40,000	$3,000	$0	$95	n/a	2/8/2014	2/4/2015
Marriott Rewards Card	Chase	Hotel	50,000	$1,000	$0	$85	n/a	2/24/2014	2/4/2015

Click The Link Below To Download My Spreadsheet To Keep Track Of Your Credit Cards, Miles & Offers

(Go to: http://bit.ly/credit-card-and-mile-tracker)

I have also heard rave reviews about using Award Wallet. Personally, I don't have all of my accounts hooked into it yet because I've found it to be cumbersome and haven't given it my full attention to connect all of my accounts. Since Award Wallet doesn't show you how they keep track of all of your data, here is a screenshot of what it looks like on the inside once you've registered.

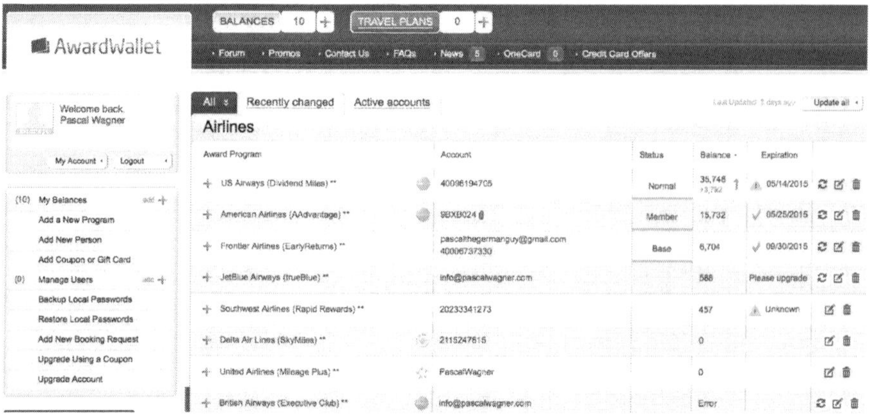

I've shown you this towards the beginning of this book, but I've also just included a tab in Excel where I just keep track of all the trips I've booked with my miles — just to keep a running tally. As of the writing of this book, I've hacked more than 10 trips, spent just under a half a million points and $715 dollars worth in taxes (most of which came from my around-the-world tour).

Trip	Starting Location	Ending Location	# of Stops	Airline	Miles	Cost
Hawaii Trip	DEN	OGG	1	United Airlines	20,000	$5.00
	OGG	DEN	3	American Airlines	17,500	$5.00
				Trip Total	**37,500**	**$10.00**
LA Zouk Congress	DEN	LAX	0	Southwest	9,251	$5.00
	LAX	DEN	0	Southwest	9,000	$0.00
				Trip Total	**18,251**	**$5.00**
Around The World	DEN			American Airlines	140,000	$633.20
		DEN				$0.00
				Trip Total	**140,000**	**$633.20**
MetaMind	DEN	PHX	0	Southwest	5,000	$8.00
	PHX	DEN	0	Southwest	7,000	$0.00
				Trip Total	**12,000**	**$8.00**
Jeff's Wedding	DEN	PIT	0	Southwest	10,000	$0.00
	PIT	DEN	0	Southwest	10,000	$5.00
				Trip Total	**20,000**	**$5.00**
Florida Weekend	DEN	SRQ	1	Delta	20,000	$5.00
	SRQ	DEN	1	Delta	20,000	$5.00
				Trip Total	**40,000**	**$10.00**
Burning Man	DEN	RNO	0	United Airlines	25,000	$0.00
	RNO	DEN	0	United Airlines	25,000	$11.20
				Trip Total	**50,000**	**$11.20**
Christmas (FL)	DEN	SRQ	2	Delta	25,000	$0.00
	SRQ	DEN	2	Delta	25,000	$11.20
				Trip Total	**50,000**	**$11.20**
Tony Robbins	DEN	LGA	0	Southwest	7,424	$5.50
	LGA	DEN	0	Southwest	7,424	$5.50
				Trip Total	**14,848**	**$11.00**
Unity Dance Festival	DEN	TPA	0	Southwest	10,484	$5.60
	TPA	DEN	0	Southwest	10,484	$5.60
				Trip Total	**20,968**	**$11.00**
				Grand Total	403,567	$715.60
				Travelhacked Trips	10	

CHAPTER 12
How To Redeem Miles
It's Not How Many You Earn, But How Much You Spend.

Now on to the fun stuff.

I almost chose to show this portion before the "how to earn miles" chapter because you should start with your destination in mind and then choose which cards suit your goals.

Why?

Flights may be cheaper using certain airlines over others.

I've taken two screenshots of flights booked to and from the same location on the same dates to illustrate how there can be a large difference in spending frequent flyer miles.

Here are two flights from Denver to Hawaii on the same dates — August 7-14, 2015.

With US Airways the total cost is 40,000 points and $62 (which you could get by opening up one credit card for 40,000 or 50,000 miles).

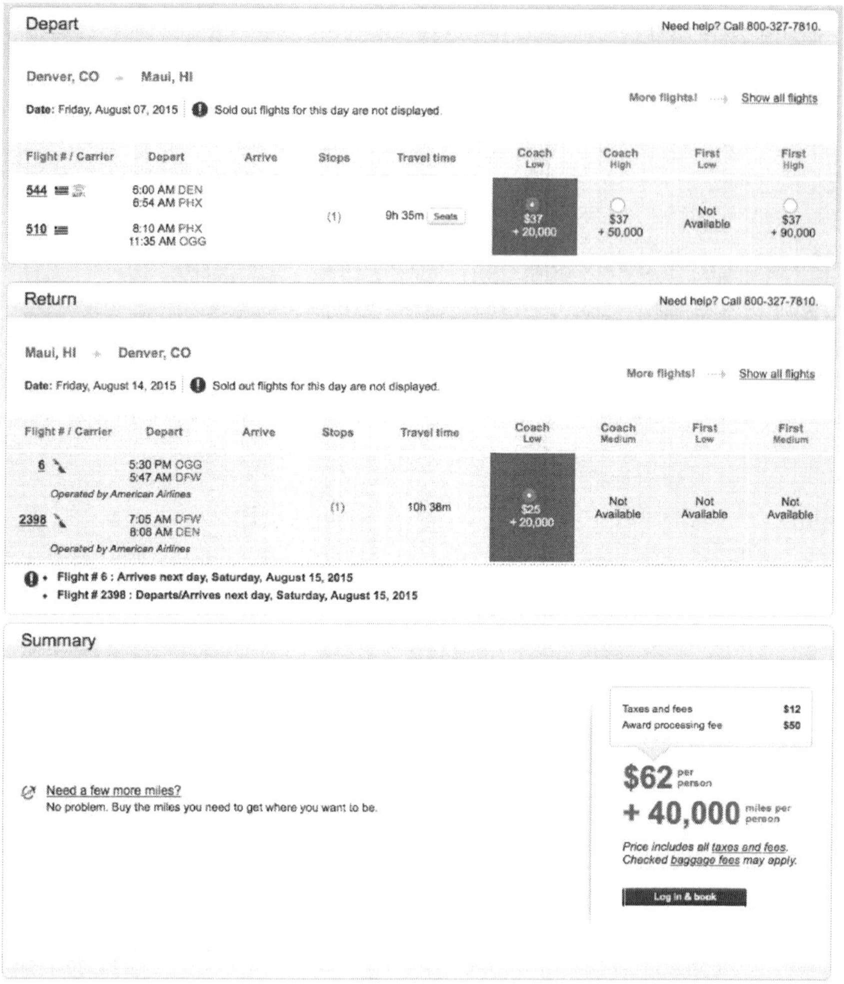

The same flight with almost all other criteria being the same, other than the airline, would cost you 60,000 frequent flyer miles and $11.20 (you would most likely need to apply for at least 2 credit cards to earn that many points).

This is just one example. Depending on your strategy you might want to save those $62 and open up another credit card, or you may determine $62 is cheap enough and that you'd rather save your other frequent flyer points.

That was just one domestic flight from Denver to Hawaii. If you tend to book flights often with award miles the differences can be astounding. I'm talking about the same flight with different carriers being more than 100,000 frequent flyer miles' difference or $1,000 more.

That's why it pays to do your research ahead of time AND THEN apply for the right credit cards.

When I first started travel hacking I made the newbie mistake of trying to outsmart all of the other bloggers who have been talking about travel hacking for years. I used the Shotgun Approach.

I applied for as many cards as I could using the fuzzy logic of "I'll figure out how to spend them when I have them. Let me just get them first." Had I just figured out how many points I would need from a specific carrier, I probably would have never applied for any Avios/British Airways credit cards. I still have yet to find a destination where I wouldn't be paying a ridiculous amount in fees *in addition* to using my points.

A trip just to London costs more than my entire around-the-world trip ticket did.

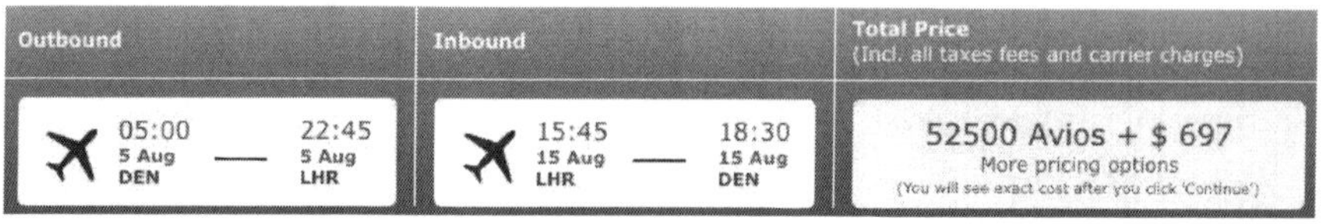

So moral of the story here is don't use the shotgun approach. Instead, spend some time researching and only apply for the cards you *need.*

The simple 3 step formula looks like this:

1. Look into the destinations you want to fly to
2. Find out which airline it is the cheapest to fly with using your frequent flyer miles
3. Apply for those credit cards that give you the points you need to book the flight

CHAPTER 13
Where To Go To Find Costs For Upcoming Trips

Just to make it clear how to do your research I've added a boatload of screenshots of various carriers. These screenshots point out exactly how to find the "book with miles" areas of their sites so you can figure out how much your dream trip is worth in miles.

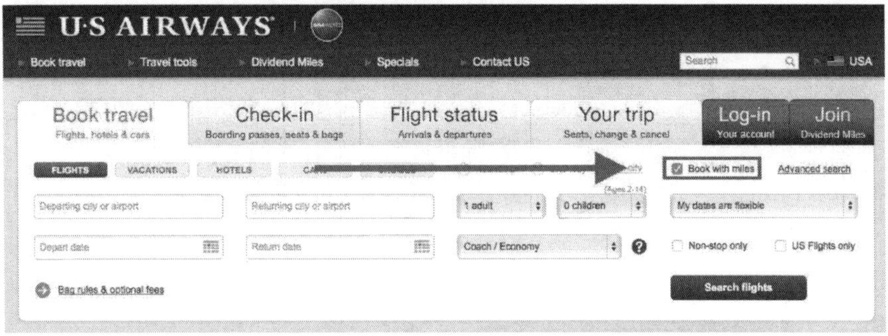

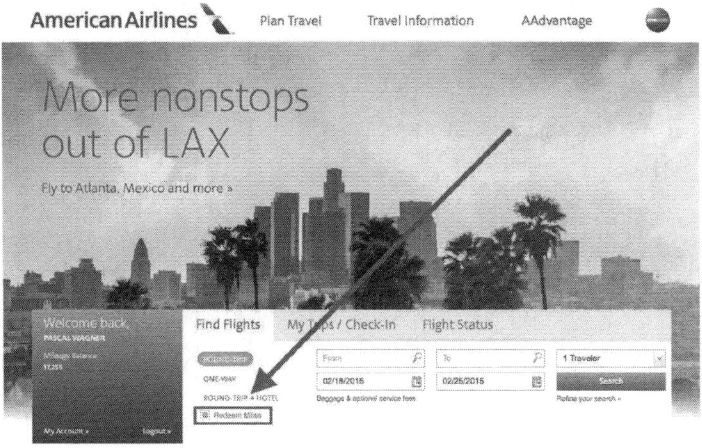

UNITED
A STAR ALLIANCE MEMBER
Home | Reservations | Travel Information | Deals & Offers | MileagePlus® | Products & Serv
Flight
Hotel
Car
Vacation
Round Trip One Way Multiple Destinations
From: (city or airport) To: (city or airport)
Search Specific Dates My Dates are Flexible
Depart Date:
Time:
9/12/2015
Anytime
Return Date:
Time:
10/12/2015
Anytime
Adults:
Children
Search By:
Price
Award Travel
Nonstop Flights Only
Advanced Search
Children, Country of Purchase...
Search
Enroll in MileagePlus®.
Learn More

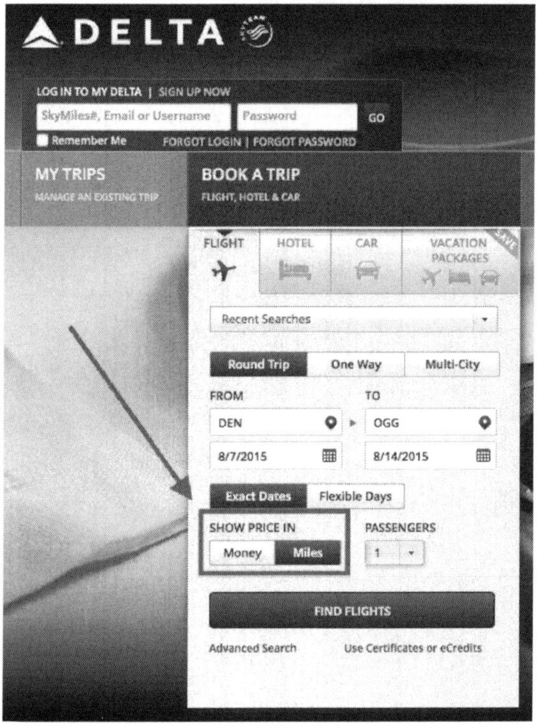
DELTA
LOG IN TO MY DELTA | SIGN UP NOW
SkyMiles#, Email or Username
Password
GO
Remember Me
FORGOT LOGIN | FORGOT PASSWORD
MY TRIPS
MANAGE AN EXISTING TRIP
BOOK A TRIP
FLIGHT, HOTEL & CAR
FLIGHT
HOTEL
CAR
VACATION PACKAGES
Recent Searches
Round Trip
One Way
Multi-City
FROM
TO
DEN
OGG
8/7/2015
8/14/2015
Exact Dates
Flexible Days
SHOW PRICE IN
Money
Miles
PASSENGERS
1
FIND FLIGHTS
Advanced Search
Use Certificates or eCredits

Where Should I Go To Apply For My Credit Cards?

There are a couple of websites dedicated to finding travel hacker-friendly cards, and almost everyone offers some way to apply for reward-oriented credit cards. Why? Because for each person that is referred by the site, the owner earns a bonus in cash or in frequent flyer miles.

Some offer better choices than others.

Here they are:

- cardsfortravel.com
- creditcards.com/airline-miles.php
- millionmilesecrets.com/hot-deals/
- thepointsguy.com/credit-cards/airline/

Around-The-World Tickets

When I first started applying for credit cards to earn the frequent flyer miles, my ultimate goal was to fly around the world. It was my holy grail of travel.

Long story short, when I was looking into my around-the-world tour tickets I found that the differences in costs was enormous. When applying for credit cards it could mean the difference between applying for three cards, or seven. Back in February 2014, this is what the going rates in frequent flyer miles were:

Economy Class — Around-The-World Ticket
United: 200,000
Delta: 180,000
American Airlines: 140,000

Obviously I chose to fly with American Airlines.

The point here is to show it pays to do your research ahead of time and figure out which airline to fly with and what cards to apply for.

Below I've included a list of a couple blog articles that do a really great job of going into detail about around-the-world tickets:

- http://bit.ly/nerdfitness-around-the-world
- http://bit.ly/oneworld-around-the-world-tickets

CHAPTER 14

How To Cancel Credit Cards And Save Your Credit

Keep Your Credit Score, Miles & Credit Line

Deciding If You Should Cancel Your Card

Now canceling your credit card is as simple as calling up your credit card company and asking them to close your account but to be a truly savvy travel hacker there is a question you should really think about before doing so:

Does the card have an annual fee?

If the answer is yes, I typically call the company and ask for a downgrade for a free card. Sometimes they offer me a couple thousand miles to remain as a customer, but if I'm going to spend another $69 or $99 annual fee it had better be for 50,000 points rather than the 5,000 they offer me to renew.

If the answer is no, I always recommend having at least a few long-term cards that you hold on to to continue building your credit history. Remember, 15% of your credit score is determined by the average age of your accounts (meaning how many years you've had each credit card open), and 30% of your credit score is determined by your credit utilization.

I now have several no-annual-fee cards that I put a monthly subscription on, like Spotify or Pandora, and have the bank automatically pay off my cards from my bank account each month. That way I'm building my credit and also using a small percentage of my credit line (something like $5 out of a $5000 credit line each month).

How To Not Lose Your Credit Line

So you've decided you are canceling your card and now, to continue building your credit score, you're looking into how to maintain and even potentially increase your credit line. You can do this in one of two ways.

When you cancel a card, you forfeit any of the credit line that you had pertaining to that card. As I've found out the hard way, banks won't reissue that cancelled line of credit to you. So that means that the best option is to transfer the credit line to one of your non-annual fee cards before canceling. Some of the banks will allow you to shift credit from one card to another before canceling. Others only allow that when you apply for a new card.

But as I mentioned, the only way I've found to increase my credit line is to either call in and ask or apply for a new credit card.

Making Sure You Don't Lose Your Points

The last part of canceling your cards is that you want to make sure that you keep all of your miles that you worked so hard to earn. Here is what you need to know about keeping your points...

Many rewards programs like Chase Ultimate Rewards, American Express Membership Rewards, and the Citi ThankYou Points are tied to whichever credit card earned them. This means that if you cancel one of these credit cards without transferring the points, there is a high likelihood that you will lose them forever. You can get around this danger by shifting the points to an account with the airline they are for. Ask your bank how to do this.

For example, if you had one of the Chase Sapphire credit cards and wanted to cancel one of them, you should transfer the ultimate rewards points that you have in your chase account to one of the frequent flyer mile programs. These are simple actions to take, but they are ones that you want to make sure you pay attention to when playing this travel hacking game.

CHAPTER 15
Next Steps & Resources

I can't tell you how long we'll be able to earn frequent flyer miles through credit cards, but what I can tell you is that this won't last forever.

At this point you should have a firm grasp of where you want to travel to and how to go about applying for the right cards to get to get to your dream destination.

The next step is to look through the credit card offers and figure out which ones you should apply for.

Below I've given you a list of different places where you can look at the credit card offers available. I recommend looking through a couple of these as certain sites might have better offers for the same credit card.

- cardsfortravel.com
- creditcards.com/airline-miles.php
- millionmilesecrets.com/hot-deals/
- thepointsguy.com/credit-cards/airline/

And in terms of additional resources, when I first started I dug into every travel blog I could find. Below I have listed many of my favorites that I believe are worth checking into. In no particular order:

- flyertalk.com
- traveladdicts.net
- travelhacking.org
- nomadicmatt.com
- thepointsguy.com
- noobtraveler.com
- frugaltravelguy.com
- cashcowcouple.com
- millionmilesecrets.com

And here are some additional articles I thought were worth checking out:

- http://bit.ly/get-busy-living
- http://bit.ly/traveling-9-to-5
- http://bit.ly/italian-fix-travel-hacking-cartel
- http://bit.ly/wisebread-travel-hacking-cartel

CHAPTER 16
It's Your Turn To Travel The World

You now have everything you need to travel the world with pennies on the dollar. Though there are several moving parts, it's definitely something you can do.

I have taught you how to plan your next free trip, starting with how to earn frequent flyer miles, and how to look into spending them.

You have also learned how this will affect your credit either positively, if you're responsible, or negatively if you're not, and how to build your credit for the long term.

All of these moving parts are the ones that you need to fly around the world and begin accumulating frequent flyer miles, but getting just a few free flights doesn't have to be the end of your journey.

As I talked about at the beginning of the book, earning flights around the world and expanding your view of the world has so much more to offer. It's only the beginning of what you will do.

Not only have I seen first-time travel hackers go from never having applied for a credit card in their lives to becoming a pro and galavanting across the earth, but I have also watched people gain the ability to live lifestyles that they love, all from just building upon this new strategy. Earning frequent flyer miles is a gateway to so many other great adventures.

If you follow what I've laid out exactly, you will earn enough frequent flyer miles to earn multiple free flights, even around the world — I guarantee it.

I wrote this book because I wanted to share what so many of us have taken advantage of in terms of next to free flights without experiencing all of the mistakes that I made early on.

Follow this exact blueprint that has already helped so many people all around the world travel to the most unique destinations.

The next step is up to you.

The key is to take action; take the first step and begin the process of applying for your cards.

Make the commitment to yourself.

Decide today that you will earn your first free flight.

If I can go from never having been on the other side of the earth to spending weeks in Thailand, Bali, Hong Kong, and Australia, so can you.

If Diego Corzo, a developer at General Motors, can earn free flights around the United States, so can you.

If Ginger Kern, an entrepreneur in Boulder, can use travel hacking to earn free flights to conferences to boost her business, so can you.

You picked up this book for a reason.

It sparked your interest because you have a desire to see the world and amazing adventures to take. Whatever your motivation is, take it on and see what the world has to offer.

It's now your turn to travel.

Regardless of whether you've already been travel hacking for years or you're getting started because of this book, I want to hear your success stories.

I hope that you will send me a note or a photo when you board your first free flight, telling me how you are doing and how your life has changed as a result of travel hacking (I'd love to feature you in the next edition of this book).

You can reach me at info@pascalwagner.com or on twitter @PascalWagner1.

Here's to your success!
Pascal Wagner

SIGN UP FOR THE FREE UDEMY COURSE ACCOMPANYING THIS BOOK!

Just to say thanks for buying or downloading my book, I would like to give you access to the Udemy Course I am putting together 100% FREE!

In video form I will walk through how to look for the best deals, exactly what you should be looking out for in credit card offers, conversations I have with credit card companies when canceling my cards, and much more that I simply wouldn't be able to explain in a book.

This course will ONLY be free to purchasers of this book and will eventually be sold to the general public at $37. So be sure to sign up as being a buyer of this book.

(Go to: http://bitly.com/free-travel-course)

THANK YOU FOR YOUR SUPPORT

Thank you for buying or downloading my book!

I really appreciate all of your feedback, and I love hearing what you have to say.

To make this book that much better for you and your friends, I'd love your input to make the next version better.

Please leave me a helpful REVIEW on Amazon.

Thanks so much!!
~ Pascal Wagner

ABOUT THE AUTHOR

Pascal Wagner

Like what you read and want to see what else I'm up to?

I do other cool things like run an event called the Elevate Mastermind, that brings together some of the top, most impactful entrepreneurs in their 20's and early 30's who are going to make a dent in the world. Our mission is to bring together these entrepreneurs to build life long and meaningful relationships through our ridiculous bucket list adventures.

Check us out at www.facebook.com/elevate-mastermind to learn about who we invite, what we do on our adventures, and potentially become someone who is invited to one of our events.

Learn about the other cool things I do at www.pascalwagner.com

20185524R00042

Made in the USA
Middletown, DE
17 May 2015